# MOTHER EARTH'S
# QUILTING
# BEE

### Appliqué Projects Inspired by
### Mother Earth and Her Children

## SIEGLINDE SCHOEN SMITH

*Breckling Press*

Library of Congress Cataloging-in-Publication Data

Schoen Smith, Sieglinde, 1941-

  Mother Earth's quilting bee : projects inspired by Mother Earth and her

children / Sieglinde Schoen Smith.

    pages cm

  ISBN 978-1-933308-30-2

1.  Quilting--Patterns. 2.  Appliqui--Patterns.  I. Olfers, Sibylle,

1881-1916. Etwas von den Wurzelkindern. Adaptation of (expression): II.

Title.


  TT835.S34848 2013

  746.46--dc23


                    2012047760

This book was set in Goudy Old Style, Cronos Pro, Carlton and Harrington
Patterns inspired by *Etwas von den Wurzelkindern* by Sibylle von Olfers, 1906
Editorial and art direction by Anne Knudsen
Interior and cover production by Maria Mann
Photography by Sharon Hoogstraten,
except photos on page 8 and pages 12 to 15 by Cathy Meals

Published by Breckling Press
283 N. Michigan St, Elmhurst, IL 60126
Printed and bound in China

International Standard Book Number (ISBN 13): 978-1-933308-30-2

I grew up in a small town in southern Germany, in the state of Wuerrtemberg. I was the second youngest of four sisters—and the troublemaker in our family. My early years were spent during a horrific period in Germany's history—the painful days of World War II. Even for young children, these were gray, ugly years. We had no toys or picture books. We almost never tasted candy or sweets of any kind. There was sadness and fear all around, even in the faces of the youngest of us. And so imagine my delight one Spring when I, little more than a toddler, made an amazing discovery. I saw flowers for the first time. I watched them peep out of the ground day by day then miraculously burst into color! Such colors I had never seen before in that place of gray lands and gloomy skies. What smiles they brought to the faces of my sisters! With the instincts of a child in search of a new toy, I played with those flowers, thrusting my little fingers into the soil and pulling them up by the roots. I wanted to find out where those magical colors came from. I would pull the flowers off their stems to see if there was a little pot of paint hiding under the blooms! My mother explained to me that flowers were God's way of working magic and tried to persuade me to leave them to grow in peace. But as I said, trouble was my middle name, and they quickly became my favorite playthings!

This collection of sewing projects celebrates flowers in all their magnificent colors and shapes. As I chose fabrics, I tried to remember the thrill of discovery when my young mind first opened to the wonders of nature around me.

*Sieglinde Schoen Smith*

# Techniques

I am a self-taught
quilter and have only recently
taken up this wonderful craft. Of course,
I learned to sew and embroider when I was
very young. My grandmother, Oma, as I called
her, helped me with my first embroidery stitches
as soon as I was able to hold a needle. From age 3
onwards, Oma would try to keep me out of
trouble by sewing little projects as gifts for
my mother and my sisters. From year to
year, my little handkerchiefs and hand-
embroidered aprons would

The image of the children sewing was my favorite in the quilt Mother Earth and Her Children. Many quilters have shared with me that it is their favorite, too. There is something charmingly innocent about this industrious little girl, busy with her needlework and working with scissors that are too large for her tiny hands.

be just a little bit better and more elaborate.

After the loss of my son Steven, I turned to quilting for comfort and to keep my hands and mind busy. I started with a simple pillow, embroidered with forget-me-nots. Soon, I adapted the same pillow design to a quilt, which, at my husband's urging, I entered into a quilt show. To my surprise, it won the handcraft award.

Needing a new project, I turned to a children's book that was my favorite as a child, *Etwas von den Wurzelkindern* which translates rather awkwardly into English as *Something About the Root Children*. A classic of German children's literature, it was written in 1906 by a young woman from an aristocratic family, Sibylle von Olfers. Soon after completing the book, she entered a holy convent. The book charmingly portrays Mother Earth's little children, asleep under the tree roots during Winter, only to awaken in the Spring and become the flowers of Summer. I still loved the rich but delicately drawn illustrations, full of flowers, butterflies, beetles, and all of God's littlest creatures. I wondered if I could transfer the entire story onto a quilt.

Now, I knew little of either traditional or modern quilting methods. I didn't have a big collection of quilter's tools. I looked at the pictures in the

# Supply Kit

When you begin a new project, things move along more smoothly if you keep a set of sewing supplies at hand. Perhaps, like me, you like keeping everything in a clear plastic tote, so that you can take your handwork with you wherever you go. Because so many people ask me which brands I prefer, I have listed some of the brands I use. But please use the fabrics, needles, and threads that you enjoy and are comfortable with.

- Tracing paper: Buy 11" x 17" sheets or larger, if you can find them

- Graphite transfer paper: Buy a roll of 18" x 36" or large sheets (available at any craft store). Do not be tempted to use any image transfer material other than graphite paper. Graphite marks wash out of fabrics easily. If you make a mistake, it is easy to dab out the error with water, then start over. For stubborn marks, put a little dishwashing detergent on a toothbrush and rub. The mark will come right out. I have tried other techniques and, believe me, with appliqués as small and delicate as mine, nothing works better than graphite transfer paper.

- Fine tip permanent markers

- Fine tip ballpoint pens

- Water-soluble fabric marker

- Appliqué needles: Choose the smallest size you can thread. I use Roxanne's size 12 betweens

- Thread to your liking: I use YLI's 100 percent silk thread, matched to the color of the appliqués

- Scissors (for cutting fabric)
- Small fine point scissors (for clipping seams and cutting threads)
- Glass head straight pins
- Ruler
- Thimble
- Batting of your preference: I like the thinnest cotton batting on the market
- Black cotton piping: I use ½" single-fold bias binding
- Embroidery hoop: I use a 4" wooden hoop. The wood holds the work better, and the small size means my under-hoop finger can reach the middle easily.
- Embroidery needles: Choose a small size, either size 10 or 11; I use John James Big Eye quilting needles, size 11 (JJ 12511)
- Single-strand embroidery floss in colors of your choosing: I prefer DMC 6-ply

There are relatively few essential items in this list, so it is easy to take your sewing kit with you for train rides, doctor's appointments, or anytime you think you may have a little extra time to sew.

book, searched out some fabrics I thought would suit the task, then sat down to work. In the pages that follow, I will do my best to describe my techniques, which are very slight variations on good old-fashioned hand-sewing methods. People tell me that modern tools and techniques make for faster, more accurate work, but I'm not convinced. I completed my quilt, which I named *Mother Earth and Her Children*, in a year and a day. When it first went on display, it won Best-in-Show at America's most prestigious quilt exhibition, International Quilt Festival. It went on to win four more national prizes the same year. Since then, I have made other quilts in a similar style that have also won major awards.

So you tell me, can traditional needlework techniques like mine help you complete a sewing project quickly, accurately, and beautifully? I hope the smaller projects in this book will persuade you to give it a try.

# Fabrics

For all the projects, I used commercially purchased batiks almost exclusively. I love the variations in color across a single piece of fabric. Batiks are perfect for recreating scenes from nature; the subtle changes in hues, shadows, and highlights mirror the thousands of shades Mother Nature gives us. I also love that batiks are so lightweight. This makes them easy to sew and quilt, even through the seam allowances necessary for appliqué. Their weave is very dense, making it possible to use tiny seam allowances.

The only non-batik fabric I use is the bright white for some of the motifs on the quilt on page 21 (detail below). I found that even the brightest white cottons looked too dull next to more colorful batiks. I searched for something with a little extra sparkle. I settled on 100 percent white polyester, which gives the shine I wanted.

When shopping for batiks, buy small quantities of as many hues as you can find. For my projects, it is better to have 50 small scraps that are all different than to have a few half yards of a handful of fabrics. Instead of choosing one yellow, choose five shades of yellow. Find as many blues, greens, tans, and browns as you can—these are Mother Nature's palette and you will always find uses for them.

Step 4 Trace design

Step 5 Place tracing on top of graphite paper; background fabric is underneath

# Using Master Templates

After buying this book, you must promise me that you will *never* cut your master templates apart. These will be your guide as you plan and carry out each project. Always keep them safe for future use. This is how best to use the master templates.

## Trace the Design

1 Take out the patterns for the project you plan to make. If they are folded, place a cloth over them and iron lightly to remove any crease marks. In order to fit them on book pages, I split some of the patterns into more than one part. I did this for the pillows and the table mats (see templates on pages 74 to 84). Photocopy these pages at their full size, line up the pattern parts where they overlap, then, using invisible tape, tape the pieces together to complete your master template. Cover with a cloth, then press lightly with an iron to make sure everything is flat and smooth.

2 Lay the pattern pieces flat on a large, sturdy surface. Make sure you have good light to work by.

3 Using invisible tape, tape together sheets of tracing paper so that you are able to cover the entire template with an inch to spare around all outer edges. Place the tracing paper over the design. If needed, tape the tracing paper to the table so that it does not shift during tracing. Smooth out any air pockets or wrinkles before taping.

4 With a firm hand and a fine-tip permanent marker, start tracing the design. First copy the larger portions of the design, such as the girls and the larger flowers or bugs. Next, trace all the details, from flowers and leaves to the individual blades of grass. (To make this easy for you to visualize, my illustrations show how to trace and transfer a simple image of the letter S.)

I prefer to complete the entire tracing, including all the tiny details, before moving on. If you are less patient and can't wait to pick up your needle to sew, just choose a small area of the design to trace and transfer to fabric. Once you have satisfied your desire to see part of the design in fabric, go back to your tracing table!

## Transfer to Background Fabric

5 When the design (or the portion of the design you are working on) is completely traced, remove the tracing and set the master template aside. Choose fabric for the background onto which you will sew the appliqués and cut it to the correct size. (Check your pattern instructions, which lists all the fabrics needed for the project.) Lay it flat and place a sheet of graphite paper on top, smooth side up. Place the tracing on top of that, right side up.

6 With a firm hand and a fine-tip ballpoint pen, draw over the lines on the tracing, transferring them as graphite marks to the fabric beneath. (Use a different color pen than the permanent marker you used to trace the pattern, so that you can easily see which lines you have drawn over and which are yet to be re-drawn.) Draw over every line, including the smallest details.

Take care to keep your master templates in a safe place. You will need them to double-check placement of the design and to make sure you have completed every detail. Keep your tracings, too—you may want to recreate portions of the quilt design on pillows, table mats or other small projects.

## Make Appliqué Templates

7 Since I use each unique motif only once, I use simple tracing paper rather than template plastic or freezer paper to make my appliqué templates. Lay a sheet of tracing paper over each motif and trace the outer lines. Eyeball a ⅛" seam allowance around all sides. Cut out the motif.

Sometimes, it may be difficult to tell from the photographs which of the smaller pieces are appliquéd and which are embroidered. As a general rule, the children's faces, hair, and hands are embroidered; their clothes are appliqué. Most of the larger flower petals and leaves are appliqué; the buds, stems, and smaller leaves are usually embroidered. Bug and beetle pieces are appliqué; the bugs' legs, feet, antennae, and portions of the wings are usually embroidery. Of course, you can embroider as much or as little as you please—the decisions are all up to you!

Step 6 Hold tracing still with one hand and trace firmly with other

Design is transferred to background fabric

Step 7 Cut out motif, leaving 1/8" seam allowance all around

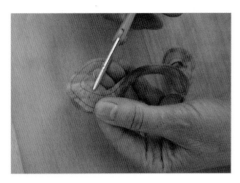

Step 8 Clip close into curves

Step 9 Pin to background fabric, exactly on top of the identical design marked there

### Sew Motifs

**8** Make sure you have added ⅛" seam allowance around all appliqué templates before cutting from fabric. At the curves, use small, sharp scissors to clip into the fabric, just two or three threads short of the stitching line, every ⅛" around the curve. This will help the sewn line lie flat.

**9** Use a single pin to attach the first appliqué motif to the background. Position the pin opposite your beginning stitching point. Use the smallest needle you can and thread in a color to match or a shade darker than your appliqué. At any clipped curves, turn under one ⅛" flap at a time. Making sure that the traced stitching line is just barely turned under, catch only a couple of threads at the edge of the motif and stitch it in place.

**10** Complete the rest of the design in the same way, using colors that please you. If you like and as you become more confident, add flowers, bugs, and butterflies of your own to make your project unique!

# Adding Embroidery

Embroidery adds a lovely, textured look that brings the children's faces to life. I use just four embroidery styles, all described here. For all embroidery, I use a single strand of DMC 6-ply embroidery floss and a size 10 or 11 needle. I recommend using a small embroidery hoop—mine is just 4" wide and is made of wood.

## Layered embroidery

Layered embroidery is the name I gave to the technique I use to embroider the children's faces and other large areas, like butterfly wings and the bodies of my little wasps. I grew up near a convent in Germany and I learned embroidery from the Sisters. My layered embroidery technique gives the children's faces a nice, soft texture; it also allows subtle shading that gives the faces natural coloring. Use single-strand embroidery floss and a stitch length of no more than ⅜."

**1** Lightly mark the area to be embroidered with lines, as shown here in blue. Use a water-soluble marker. This will help keep all your stitches going in the same direction.

**2** Begin at one end of the area to be embroidered and make a very dense row of even-sized satin stitches across to the other end. Get the stitches as close together as you can.

**3** Make a second row adjacent to the first. Do not allow a gap to show between the two rows; to achieve this smooth effect, the ends of your stitches will jut between the stitches in the first row. Use the same color or, if the design requires a new color, change thread. (In the sample shown, I started the second row with pink, then switched back to cream when I reached the end of the cheek line.)

**4** Make a third row, this time stitching over the "seam" between the first and second rows. Your stitches will sink down into the previous layers, blending invisibly into them.

Continue adding rows, overlapping each "seam" with a same-color layer and alternating colors as necessary until the design area is filled. The trick to layered embroidery is to fool the eye to the point where you can no longer distinguish the rows of embroidery but see only one continuous surface. Keeping your stitches very close together and avoiding any gaps between the rows will help.

Steps 1 and 2

Step 3

Step 4

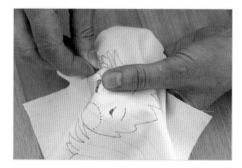

Hand position for embroidery stitch

Step 5

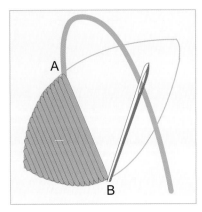

Satin stitch

## Satin Stitch

I use simple satin stitch to fill buds, leaves, stems or other small or narrow areas.

**1** Make sure the area you want to fill is clearly marked. You will work from left to right and from top to bottom of the leaf or bud.

**2** Knot the thread, then come up at A, slanting the needle at an angle. Go down at B, then up again at A, slanting the needle so that you are exiting just to the right of the previous stitch. Continue across the area to be covered, gradually increasing then decreasing the size of the stitches as the design dictates. Butt the stitches as close together as you can.

**3** If desired, work a second layer of stitches over the first to fill any gaps and create a thick, smooth pad of stitches.

## French Knot

I use French knots for details like flower buds, the eyes of butterflies, and the balls at the ends of a dragonfly's antennae. I sometimes use French knots in place of quilting, pushing the needle through all layers (see page 48).

**1** Knot the thread, then bring the needle up through the fabric from the back at an angle. If you prefer a denser knot, use double-strand floss rather than single strand.

**2** With your left thumb, hold the thread taut against the fabric, about ½" away from the entry point. Twist the needle around that ½" length of thread two or three times (depending on the size of knot you want).

**3** Push the needle back through the fabric, very close to but not into the entry point.

**4** When the needle exits at the back of the fabric, move to the spot where you want to place the next French knot, bring the needle up again, and repeat from Step 2.

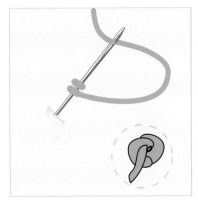

French knot

## Cross Stitch

I use cross stitch for simple decoration on the girl's dresses. I have also used single cross stitches in place of quilting, pushing the needle through all layers (see photo below).

**1** To make a single cross stitch, knot the thread, then bring the needle straight up through the fabric at your starting point, A. Go back down at B, laying the thread at a diagonal, and come up again at C. Go back down at D, laying the thread at a diagonal and over the first thread.

**2** If you are making a row of cross stitches, work from left to right. First, make a row of slanted stitches, coming up at A, going down at B, coming up at C, and continuing until you have a full row of slanted stitches.

**3** For the next stitch, come up as usual at C, but this time angle the thread to the left, laying it diagonally over the previous stitch and forming an x. Continue working from right to left until you have a row of neat crosses.

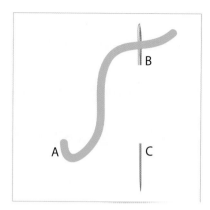

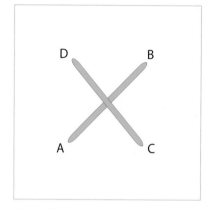

Step 1 Single cross stitch

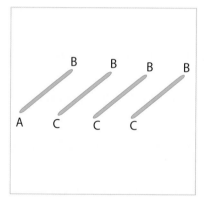

Step 2 Make row of slanted stitches

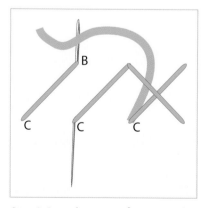

Step 3 Complete row of cross stitch

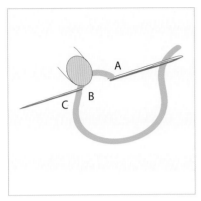

Step 1 Make a loop

Steps 2 and 3 Complete lazy daisy

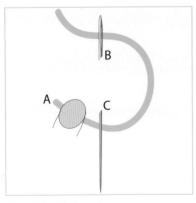

Step 2 Hold thread

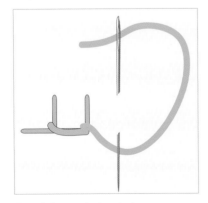

Step 3 Buttonhole stitch

## Lazy Daisy Stitch

Sometimes I use a simple lazy daisy stitch to embellish flower centers (see below, left).

**1** Knot the thread, then bring the needle up through the fabric from the back. Come up at A and make a small loop, holding it against the fabric with your left thumb. Go down as close as possible to A, but not into it. Do not pull the loop through the fabric.

**2** Come up at B and make a small stitch over the loop, (to C) holding it in place. Bring the needle back up at A. Repeat, making a second lazy daisy stitch.

**3** Continue working from center point A until you have made a lazy daisy stitch flower.

## Buttonhole Stitch

I use a tiny buttonhole stitch for the collars on some of the dresses and for additional flower decorations (see below, left).

**1** This stitch is worked from left to right. Knot the thread and bring the needle up through the fabric from the back.

**2** Come up at A. Holding the thread down with your thumb then looping it as shown, go down at B. Then, holding the needle flat, come up at C.

**3** Lay the thread to the right and repeat the previous step until you have created a line of stitches.

Buttonhole stitch, lazy daisy stitch, and black stem stitch

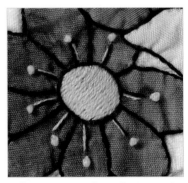

Yellow satin stitch , yellow French knots, and black stem stitch

## Outlining with Stem Stitch

Once all the appliqué and embroidery is complete, I outline each motif in black with stem stitch embroidery. I stitch around the embroidered faces and bugs as well as around the fabric appliqués. I also use stem stitch for drawing the antennae of butterflies, spider webs, and other fine details. Outlining not only help the motifs stand out crisp against the background, but it covers any less-than-perfect appliqué stitches!

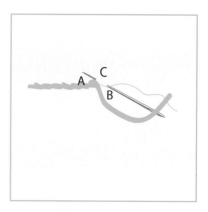

Stem stitch

1 Work as close as possible to the edge of the appliqué motif, but stitch into the background, not the motif. Knot the thread, then bring the needle up from the back to the front at you starting point (A).

2 Make a slant stitch about ⅛" long to B, then re-insert the needle, angling it back toward A.

3 Come up at C, about half way along the previous stitch. Repeat, continuing around the entire motif. Exit at the back of the work and knot off.

Stem stitch is used to outline every element of the design as well for stitching several details

# Quilting Bee

"All are quick and ever ready,
To sew spring clothes, their hands are steady.
With needles, scissors, spools of thread,
They measure and cut, full steam ahead."

How many happy hours I spent as a child,
working on scraps from Mama's sewing basket!
When the weather permitted, my sisters
and I would make our own little sewing
circle outside, in the midst of woodland
flowers. I would sit patiently
watching my sisters
weave

Finished size: 40½" x 40½", including binding

Quilting Bee

# Materials

All quantities are generous so that you can cut large shapes from a single piece of fabric, wherever possible. You will have plenty of leftover fabric to play with! For the background, cameo backgrounds, and most appliqués, I use cotton batiks. The slight color variation across the yardage lends a natural feel that is in keeping with the style of the quilt.

## Background

**Sky:** 1 yard light blue

**Border:** 4 yards of border print fabric with stripe; or 1 yard plain fabric

**Cameo backgrounds:** ¼ yard cream (notice that there are tints of pink, orange, yellow, and lilac in the cream batik scraps I chose); ¼ yard green, scraps of brown

**Cameo borders:** ½ yard bright green or ¼ yard each of two shades of green (you will have leftover fabric once borders are cut). (If you choose the same green used for the cameo backrounds, there is no need to purchase additonal fabric)

## Appliqués

**Dresses:** ⅛ yard each of purple, white, gold, dark blue, light yellow, magenta, red, light blue, orange, pink, and lilac (see my note on page 11 about choosing a bright white)

**Shoes/socks:** Scraps of brown, black, and white

**Foliage:** Scraps in at least five shades of green

**Insects:** Scraps in shades of brown, purple, rust, orange,

**Flowers, bugs and butterflies:** Scraps in as many colors as you can find!

**Letters:** Scraps in a variety of colors

## Plus

**Backing:** 1 ½ yards, any color

**Batting:** 1 yard very thin batting (see *Sieglinde's Secret* on page 35)

**Binding:** 5 yards single-fold bias binding

**Embroidery:** Single-ply embroidery thread in black and white, as well as shades of silver, grey, gold, yellow, orange, brown, cream, pink, lilac, teal, and whatever additional colors you please

**Delica beads:** About 450 beads in a variety of colors

*Note:* See page 11 for help choosing fabrics.

their colorful threads into tiny blossoms and butterflies. Soon, I was watching pretty embroidered flowers fly from my own needle, too!

Shortly after viewing my quilt, *Mother Earth and Her Children*, at Houston's International Quilt Market, Jinny Beyer invited me to teach at her studio in Great Falls, Virginia. It was a great honor for me, an unknown quilter, to be invited by the quilting world's most celebrated designer. Even though our quilting styles and color palettes are very different, Jinny challenged me to come up with the sampler design that could incorporate one of her popular border print fabrics. You can see it in the border of *The Quilting Bee*. This quilt is dedicated to Jinny Beyer, with heartfelt thanks for the inspiration and guidance she has given and continues to give to today's quilters.

# Make Cameo Backgrounds

**1** Begin with the center cameo. Cut a circle from cream fabric, measuring 9" diameter. Cut a half-circle from green measuring 9½" diameter. On the template, identify the line between the cream sky and the green grass. Since most of the grass edge is hidden by appliqués, you will need to visualize where the line runs from left to right across the cameo. Transfer this line onto both cream and green fabrics. Next, transfer the lines of the curved green border (both inner and outer lines) onto both the cream and green fabrics (see page 13 for help on transferring the design). Rough cut the cream and green fabrics to an approximate size first, then carefully trim each piece so that there is an even ⅛" seam allowance around the exact shapes you need. Note that the grass and the cameo border can be cut as a single piece. Make sure you leave ⅛" seam allowance on either side of the cameo border. Appliqué the upper edge of the green grass piece on top of the cream sky piece, tucking under the green seam allowance and clipping curves as you go. Do the same around the entire inner border, leaving the upper left, quadrant unstitched for now (it will be stitched once the tree trunk and branches are appliquéd in place in Step 4). You will need to clip curves as you sew, so that the green piece lies nice and flat on top of the cream fabric. (See page 13 for help with appliqué.) Turn the piece over and, with sharp scissors, cut away any excess cream fabric from beneath the large green grass piece. This will reduce bulk and make the next round of stitching easier.

**2** For the remaining four cameo backgrounds, cut four cream circles measuring 7" diameter and four green half circles measuring 7" diameter. Cut four strips of brown fabric (one for each cameo) measuring 1" x 5¼". If you wish, use varying shades of brown. As before, transfer the line that separates the sky from the grass onto both cream and green fabrics, checking against the master template to make sure they match. Next, transfer the lines around the brown area onto both the brown and green fabrics. Rough cut the cream and green fabrics to an approximate size first, then carefully trim each piece so that there is an even ⅛" seam allowance around the exact shape you need and on either side of the green border. Carefully cut into the green fabric, cutting out the shape marked for the brown piece (leaving about ⅛" seam allowance). Appliqué the green piece on top of the brown, tucking under the green seam allowance as you go. Appliqué the upper edge of the green grass piece on top of the cream sky piece, tucking under the green seam allowance. Do the same around the entire inner border. You will need to clip curves as you sew, so that the green piece lies neatly on top of the cream fabric. (See page 13 for help with appliqué.) Turn the piece over and, with sharp scissors, cut away any excess cream fabric from beneath the large green grass appliqué. Trim off any excess brown fabric, too.

# Transfer Cameo Designs

**3**  Trace and transfer all the motifs and designs in the center cameo onto your piece of green/cream background fabric from Step 1. Following the directions on page 12, trace carefully to make sure you catch every single detail. Continually check against the master template to ensure accuracy.  In the same way, trace and transfer the motifs and designs for the other four cameos onto your pieces of green/cream/brown background fabrics from Step 2.

# Center Cameo

**4**  Working from left to right, cut pieces (adding a ⅛" seam allowance) for the light brown tree, the dark brown knot in the tree, the orange, pink, and lilac dresses, the black shoe, and the blue fabric. (Note that the children's faces, hair, and hands, plus the leaves and flowers are embroidered; you will not have to cut appliqués for these pieces.) Appliqué each piece in place, following the exact design you traced onto the background fabric in Step 3. Appliqué the knot first, followed by the tree. Next, appliqué the orange dress, the black shoe, the pink dress, the blue fabric, and, last, the lilac dress. Appliqué the unsewn section of border over the edge of the tree trunk. Turn the work over and trim away any excess fabric to reduce bulk.

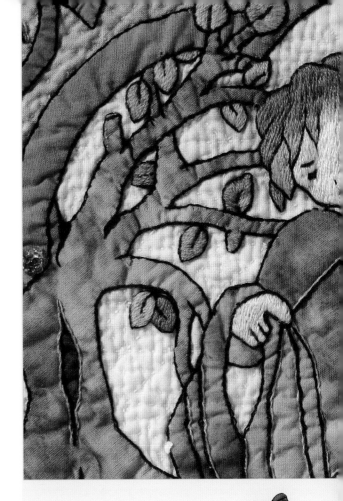

## Sieglinde's Secret

*I prefer to completely finish tracing and transferring the image to fabric before I begin any sewing. If you are less patient and can't wait to pick up your needle, complete the main figures in the design, such as the children's bodies. Next, choose another distinct area of the design to concentrate on, such as one of the faces or a clump of flowers. Mark your chosen area completely, then start sewing. When you are done, move on to another distinct area of the design.*

"And when the children's clothes are done,
Kind Mother Earth admires each one."

**5**  Complete the layered embroidery of the children's faces, hair, necks, and hands. (For help with layered embroidery, see page 14.) With black thread, carefully add the children's eyes, brows, mouths, and lips, as in the photograph. Complete the embroidery of the leaves and flowers using simple satin stitch (see page 16). Use stem stitch and green thread to embroider the blades of grass (see page 19). Note that one of the leaves on the tree overlaps the cameo border; leave this portion until the cameo is sewn to the quilt background.

**6**  With single-strand black embroidery thread and stem stitch, outline all elements of the design. Begin by outlining the inner and outer edges of the border. Outline the dark brown knot in the tree trunk. Outline around each child's body, face, hair, and hands. Add extra lines of stem stitch to the hair of the girl dressed in lilac. Add lines of black stem stitch to delineate the children's arms, as in the photograph. Do the same to delineate the thread in the hand of the girl in orange. On the blue fabric, add lines of stem stitch to delineate fabric folds. Outline the tree and each flower and leaf.  Add a line of black stem stitch next to each blade of grass. Study the photograph to see exactly where to outline.

**7**  With single-strand pink embroidery thread, add a line of stem stitch next to the black line that delineates the arm of the girl in pink. Do the same with lilac thread for the girl in lilac and orange thread for the girl in orange. Add a line of blue outline stitch alongside the black stitches on the blue fabric. Add lines of gold stem stitch along the thread held by the girl in orange and around the hair of the girl in lilac.

All four other cameos are constructed in the same way, as detailed on the pages that follow. If you need to, refer back to this section for extra help. The photographs will show you exactly where to sew and what colors to use. Once you get into the swing of things, you may decide to simplify the design to make it easier to sew or vary it to make it unique. See how talented you are!

## Sieglinde's Secret

*Practice always makes perfect! Quilters I have met tell me they are often nervous about sketching the children's faces onto fabric. My advice is to keep a sketchbook or a few cut pieces of muslin on hand and pull them out whenever you have downtime during the day. Practice sketching eyes, eyebrows, noses and mouths. Look at pictures of young children or watch their smiling faces as they play. You'll be surprised how quickly your sketching improves! And you'll also find that any errors you make are easily covered with embroidery stitches.*

# Top Cameo

**8** Adding ⅛" seam allowances, cut yellow and white pieces for the sun, two pieces for the dark purple dress, a piece for the dusty pink fabric, two brown pieces for the shoes, and a tiny white piece for the sock. Appliqué the tiny sock piece first, followed by the dark purple dress pieces, the dusty pink fabric pieces, and the shoes. Appliqué the white then the yellow sun pieces. Turn the work over and trim away any excess fabric to reduce bulk.

**9** Follow Steps 5 to 6 above and study the photograph to complete all of the embroidery in the correct colors. Use silver or gray thread for the scissors. Use tiny buttonhole stitches and French knots for the girl's collar and buttons (see pages 16 and 18). Follow Step 7 to outline each element of the design in black embroidery thread.

*Note that the girl's face and hands, the white triangles in the sun, the scissors, and all the leaves and flowers are embroidered; you will not have to cut appliqués for these pieces.*

# Right Cameo

**10** Adding ⅛" seam allowances, cut two pieces for the yellow dress, a piece for the orange fabric, a brown piece for the shoe, and a tiny white piece for the sock. Appliqué the tiny sock piece first, followed by the yellow dress pieces, the orange fabric piece, and the shoe. Turn the work over and trim away any excess fabric to reduce bulk.

**11** Follow Steps 5 to 6 above and study the photograph to complete all of the embroidery in the correct colors. Use tiny buttonhole stitches for the girl's collar. Add delica beads for her buttons. Follow Step 7 to outline each element of the design in black embroidery thread.

*Note that the girl's face and hands and all the leaves and flowers are embroidered; you will not have to cut appliqués for these pieces.*

# Bottom Cameo

**12** Adding ⅛" seam allowances, cut two pieces for the magenta dress, two pieces for the gold fabric, a brown piece for the shoe, and a tiny white piece for the sock. Appliqué the tiny sock piece first, followed by the magenta dress pieces, the gold fabric pieces, and the shoe. Turn the work over and trim away any excess fabric to reduce bulk.

**13** Follow Steps 5 to 6 above and study the photograph to complete all embroidery in the correct colors. Decorate the girl's collar, cuff, and hem with a combination of embroidery stitches of your choice (see page 14). Add three delica beads for the buttons. Follow Step 7 to outline each element of the design in black embroidery thread.

*Note that the girl's face and hands, her sock, and all the leaves, flowers and butterfly are embroidered; you will not have to cut appliqués for these pieces.*

# Left Cameo

**14** Adding ⅛" seam allowances, cut two pieces for the light blue dress, one piece for the dark blue fabric, and two brown pieces for the shoes. Appliqué the light blue dress pieces first, followed by the dark blue fabric piece and the shoes. Turn the work over and trim away any excess fabric to reduce bulk.

**15** Follow steps 5 to 6 above and study the photograph to complete all of the embroidery in the correct colors. Add tiny buttonhole stitches for the collar and three delica beads for the buttons. Follow Step 7 to outline each element of the design in black embroidery thread.

*Note that the girl's face and hands and all the leaves and flowers embroidered; you will not have to cut appliqués for these pieces.*

## Add Beaded Flowers

**16** Add delica bead flowers to the borders of each cameo (center cameo has 7; top cameo has 7; right cameo has 8; bottom cameo has 8; left cameo has 6). For each, stitch a colored center bead in place first. Without cutting the thread, string 8 delica beads in a complimentary color onto it and arrange them around the center bead. (Depending on the size of your center bead, you may need one more or one less delica.) Secure in place with one or two stitches between every couple of beads. Set the completed cameos aside for now.

## Prepare the Quilt Background

**17** Cut a single piece of blue background fabric to measure 33" x 33". This leaves a ¼" seam allowance around all sides. Cut 8 narrow border strips measuring 9¼" x 2" (this includes ¼" seam allowance). Cut 4 narrow border strips measuring 15¼" x 2". Make a diagonal cut across the short edges of each strip, checking against the master template to make sure each strip is the exact shape you need (plus ¼" seam allowance).

**18** Take two of the shorter strips from Step 17. Right sides in, pin together at the diagonal. Miter the corner by sewing across the diagonal, using a ¼" seam allowance. Open the seam and press. Repeat for all four corners.

**19** Take the corner piece from Step 18 and one of the longer strips from Step 17. Fold then press a ¼" seam allowance along each long edge of the corner strip and the long strip. Press. Pin each strip in place onto the corners of the background fabric. Make sure the ¼" seam allowance of the background fabric extends beyond your positioned border strips. Appliqué both long edges of the corner piece onto the blue background first. Appliqué the diagonal strip, sewing over and hinding the short raw edges of the corner strip Leave the short edges of the diagonal strip unsewn, as they will be covered by the quilt border. Repeat for all four corners.

## Sieglinde's Secret

*Since I designed this quilt in honor of Jinny Beyer (see page 23), I decided to use one of her popular print fabrics for the borders. If you are using a decorative border print, take care to "fussy cut" your strips so that any motif or pattern in the design matches up perfectly when the miters at the corner are sewn together.*

**20** Follow the directions on page 13 to transfer all the motifs on the blue background onto fabric. Start by drawing a line ¼" in from the edge around all four sides of the fabric piece. This is the seam allowance. Trace the complete pattern onto tracing paper first, then use graphite paper to transfer the design to fabric. Work carefully, tracing one section at a time until there entire design is transferred to fabric in full detail.

## Add Cameos

**21** Pin then appliqué each of the completed cameos in place onto the quilt background. Carefully tuck in the green border fabric seam allowance as you go, clipping curves as necessary. Complete the leaf embroidery that overlaps the border of the center cameo.

## Add Lettering

**22** Follow the directions on page 13 to transfer the letters spelling *Quilting Bee* in place around the center cameo. Trace the letters onto tracing paper first, then use graphite paper to transfer the marks to fabric. Work carefully, tracing one letter at a time. Complete any portions of the design that fall within the letters, such as the embroidered spider and web, the embroidered butterfly, and the tiny embroidered flowers and appliqué leaf inside the letter Q. Use stem stitch in black and green to embroider the blades of grass, too (see page 19).

## Complete Appliqués

**23** Cut the fabrics for the dresses and socks of the three children at top right of the quilt. Cut pieces for the flowers, stems, and leaves they are holding. (Note that the yellow flowers, the green patch on the white flower, and the butterfly body, legs, and antennae are embroidered so no fabric pieces are needed.) Appliqué the dresses in place first. Look carefully at the photographs of each child to decide the best sequence for appliqué/embroidery. For instance, for the girls in white and purple, the faces and hair will need to be embroidered before

## Sieglinde's Secret

*Perhaps you would like to appliqué a child's name or a special message onto your quilt, instead of the words* Quilting Bee. *For additional letters, refer to my book* Mother Earth's ABC, *which includes every letter of the alphabet, upper case and lower case. For a super-quick way to transfer letters, I have also published* Mother Earth's ABC: Phototransfer Pack & CD. *Use this to digitally print letters onto fabric sheets. Look at the back of the book for more information on both these products.*

*Notice how the embroidery stitching on motifs like the frog and the centipide really bring these little critters to life!*

the stems are sewn in place. For all the children, the hands are embroidered last.  (For help with layered embroidery for the hair and faces, see page 14.) Cut fabric for the wings of the butterfly above the head of the girl in white (the rest of the butterfly is embroidered).  Use black embroidery thread and stem stitch to outline each figure, leaf, flower, etc. Use outline stitch and other embroidery in whatever colors you wish to add details to each figure (such as sleeves, necklace, patterns on dress, etc). Sew two rows of delica beads to each pink wing of the butterfly (about 40 beads). Use stem stitch and black and green thread to embroider the blades of grass in this area of the quilt.

24   Cut fabrics for the dress, socks, and shoes of the girl at bottom left. In addition, cut pieces for the fabric she is holding and the critters that surround her. (Note that the small butterflies in front of the girl are embroidered, so no fabric pieces are needed. The bees' bodies and the bodies of the other two butterflies are also embroidered, as are the eyes of the snail and the frog.) Appliqué the girl's socks and shoes in place first, followed by the dress, then the basket. Study the photographs to decide the best sequence for appliqué/embroidery of each shape. (For help with layered embroidery for the girl's hair and face, see page 14.) Use black embroidery thread and stem stitch to outline each figure, bug, etc. Use outline stitch and other embroidery in whatever colors you wish to add details to each figure (such as sleeves, neck-lace, patterns on dress and basket). Sew two rows of delica beads to the bottom of the dress (about 35 beads) and four beads for buttons at the neck. Use stem stitch and black and green thread to embroider the blades of grass in this area of the quilt.

25   Next, work on the cluster of bugs and beetles at the bottom right of the quilt. If you have not done so already, trace the shapes then use graphite paper to transfer the marks to fabric (see pages 12 to 13). Look carefully at the photographs to determine the best sequence in which to appliqué/embroi-der each bug. Notice that all the legs, antennae, and eyes are embroidered, as are the bee's body, the snail's body, the spots on the ladybug and toadstools, the butterfly body, and the pattern on its wings. Outline each bug and add details to the bodies with stem stitch and black embroidery thread (see page 19). Use stem stitch and black and green thread to embroider the blades of grass in this area of the quilt.

**26** Move to the top left of the quilt and work on the large cluster of flowers, the two butterflies, and the bee. If you have not done so already, trace the shapes then use graphite paper to transfer the marks to fabric (see page 13). Look carefully at the photographs to determine the best sequence in which to appliqué/embroider each flower or bug. Notice that the tiny yellow flower buds and flower centers are embroidered, as are the bodies, legs, and antennae of the bee and butterflies. Most of the thinner flower stems are embroidered, too. Outline each flower or bug and add details to the bodies with stem stitch and black embroidery thread (see page 19). Add delica beads as desired to embellish the orange, red, and pink flowers. Use stem stitch and black and green thread to embroider the blades of grass in this area of the quilt.

**27** Next, work on the design inside each corner triangle. With the exception of the bees's wings, both top triangles are entirely embroidered. Both bottom triangles are entirely appliqué. If you have not done so already, trace the shapes then use graphite paper to transfer the marks to fabric (see page 13). Look carefully at the photographs to determine the best sequence in which to appliqué/embroider. Outline each shape and add details with stem stitch and black embroidery thread (see page 19). Use stem stitch and black and silver embroidery thread to create the spider web in the top right triangle.

**28** Lay your tracings over the quilt and make sure there are no design motifs or details you have missed. Check against the master template, too. Make sure every motif is outlined with black embroidery thread.

Now your quilt top is ready for the borders, backing and final quilting. This is your last chance to make sure you *love* your design. If you feel there are blank spaces, why not add an extra flower or another little bug, bee, or beetle? Lay out your quilt top only a clear surface and leave it for a few days so that you are certain it is finished and as perfect as it can be.

If you were able to look at the back of one of my appliqué projects, you would see that I leave many areas unquilted. Rather than struggle with appliqué seams, I quilt only the  open areas of the background, between and around the motifs. Keep this in mind as you begin to quilt your project in the next section.

## Sieglinde's Secret

*I quilt with Mettler cotton thread to match the fabric. Use a needle that is comfortable for you. I like to use the smallest, finest needles that fit the thread used. The smaller the needle the easier the needle glides through the fabric. I also use Thread Heaven thread conditioner and protectant.*

*Because batik fabrics, which I used for the background, the cameos, and the appliqués, are hard to needle, I always use the thinnest batting I can find. My preference is Mountain Mist's 100 percent cotton batting, which needles very easily.*

# Add Borders

**29** Since sewing on so many appliqués can slightly change the size of the background fabric you are working with, measure your quilt across the center, horizontally and vertically. Cut vertical and horizontal borders at lengths to match these measurements, plus ½" for seam allowances (about 33", but check to make sure.) The width of each strip will be 4½", including seam allowance.

**30** Carefully pin each border to the quilt top, right sides facing, then sew in place using ¼" seam allowance. Use the miter triangle on page 85 to cut miters on each end of each horizontal and each vertical border. Align as shown in the diagram, taking care to leave ¼" seam allowance.

**31** Cut narrow border strips to fit the diagonal across each corner of the quilt. Make sure you measure each corner accurately before you cut. You may find that your four corners are not exactly the same size; when a quilt top is so heavily appliquéd, it is not unusual for the background fabric to stretch. The border strip measurement will be roughly 11½" x 1¾" (this includes ¼" seam allowances). Right sides together, pin then sew the border strips to each corner of the quilt, using ¼" seam allowance.

**32** If desired, run a line of stem stitch in black thread along the seams that join the borders to the quilt top. Run another line of stem stitch along the narrow triangle borders at each corner.

# Add Backing

**33** Check the size of your quilt again, measuring across the center, horizontally and vertically. Cut a rectangle of backing fabric that matches these measurements, plus an extra inch on all sides. For this quilt, the rectangle will be about 41½" x 41½", but measure to make sure. Cut a layer of batting with the same measurements. Trim the diagonal corners of both backing and batting to match the corners of the quilt top.

**34** Lay out the backing on a table top, and position the batting then the quilt top over it, smoothing each layer out as you go. Pin the layers together, using one pin at least every square inch. Baste the entire quilt and remove the pins.

# Quilting

**35** The quilting pattern for all the open areas around the appliqués and inside the cameos is a ⅜" grid crossed twice diagonally. I usually quilt without marking, but if you need to, lightly mark the pattern onto the open areas of the quilt top using a water-soluble marker. Do not quilt over the appliqués or the embroidery. The wide border is quilted with a simple ⅜" square grid.

# Binding

**36** Cut a 2" bias strip of fabric. Sew bias pieces together to form one long strip, long enough to go all around the outside edge of the quilt. Fold the strip in half lengthwise and press, matching the raw edges exactly. Leave about a 3" to 4" unfolded at one end.

**37** By hand or machine, start to attach the folded end of the strip to the top edge of the front of the quilt. Sew around the front of the quilt and around each diagonal corner.

**38** Once you get to about 4" to 6" from the end, open the bias strip. Measure how much of the strip is still needed. Trim to the correct length, plus ¼". Turn that ¼" under, fold in half again and fingerpress. Sew the end in place, slightly overlapping the starting point.

**39** Fold the unsewn long edge of the bias toward the back of the quilt and attach with small appliqué stitches.

If you need more help with finishing, basting, quilting, and binding refer to one of the many quilting books devoted to this topic. Some excellent sources are listed on page 86. If you plan to display your quilt, attach a sleeve so that you can hang it. And don't forget to attach a label with your name and date, so that everyone can know how clever you are!

# Spring Fling

"And when fair Spring arrives on time,
A merry group soon comes alive.
Ladybugs, lilies, tall blades of grass,
Emerge on the earth in a joyous mass!"

When I was little, Spring was my favorite season of the year. The first days of Spring were my chance to get outdoors and watch the world come alive after its long Winter sleep. As always, my grandmother, Oma, was in charge of keeping me out of trouble. When Spring beckoned

Finished size: 15" x 15" (teal pillow); 15 ½" x 15 ½" (off-white and pink/green pillows)

"Sleepy children open their eyes.
They stretch and yawn with soft, slow smiles."

# Materials

All quantities are generous so that you can cut large shapes from a single piece of fabric, wherever possible. You will have plenty of leftover fabric to play with! For the background and appliqués of all three pillow designs I use cotton batiks. The slight color variation across the yardage lends a natural feel that is in keeping with the style of the project.

## All Three Pillow Cases

**Pillow case (front & back):** ½ yard per pillow (you will have leftover fabric)

## Design

**Appliqués:** Large scraps for dress and letter (optional); small scraps in multiple colors for flowers and bugs
**Embroidery:** Single-ply embroidery thread in cream, light brown, dark brown, tan, beige, black, gold, pink, yellow, green, red, orange, magenta, lilac, and whatever additional colors you please

## Plus

**Closure:** Three buttons or three ½" squares of Velcro
**Thin batting:** ¼ yard per pillow
**Pillow form or batting:** Purchase or recycle standard size square pillow or stuff pillow case with batting

Note that the three pillows photographed are slightly different in size. You can modify the size as you please, or even use a purchased pillow cover. Make sure any pillow cover you purchase is made from quality fabric that needles easily.

You do not need to make your pillows identical to mine. For example, you may want to add the checkered border to the cream pillow, or you may want to add more or fewer flowers to your design. Remember, all the choices are yours to make.

*Note:* See page 11 for help in choosing fabrics.

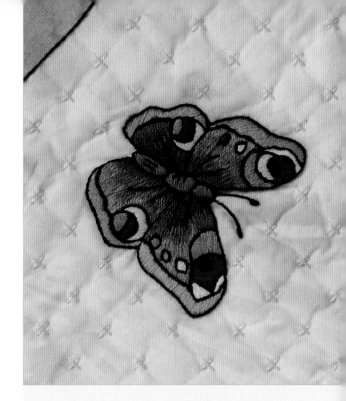

but it was still to cold outside for me to have free run of the woods and meadows, Oma would try to rein me in. I loved her so much I would do most anything to keep that dear lady smiling. Oma's sewing kit fascinated me. It was full of colorful threads which, before my innocent eyes, she could transform into the most delicate embroideries of flowers, butterflies, and bumblebees. She could turn the drab, dreary fabrics available those days into the prettiest little dresses, with Spring bouquets floating at the hems and cuffs. One day, when I was a big girl of three years old, she called me to sit with her. I scooted my little footstool next to her with much anticipation. Was Oma going to read to me or maybe tell me one of her stories? Imagine my surprise when Oma gave me a small piece of embroidery canvas and a blunt needle, threaded with pretty pink floss, then proceeded to show me how to make my first stitches.

Note that the girl's face, neck and hair are embroidered, not appliquéd. So are the bumblebee, the
butterfly, many of the smaller green leaves, and many of the flower centers. Look carefully at the
photograph to see which pieces are embroidered; you will not need to cut appliqués for these pieces.

# Cut Fabric for Pillow

**1** All cutting measurements below include ¼" seam allowance. If you prefer to work with ⅛" seam allowance, reduce the sizes accordingly.

## Off-White Pillow

Cut a square of fabric for the pillow front measuring 16" x 16"

Cut a square of thin batting measuring 15 ½" x 15 ½"

Cut another square of fabric measuring 16" x 16" (this fabric is the backing for the pillow front; it will be inside the pillow and will not be visible)

Cut a rectangle of backing fabric measuring 16" x 15"

Cut a rectangle of backing fabric measuring 16" x 4 ½"

## Teal Pillow

Cut a square of fabric and a square of thin batting measuring 16 ½" x 16 ½"

Cut another square of fabric measuring 16 ½" x 16 ½" (this fabric is the backing for the pillow front; it will be inside the pillow and will not be visible)

Cut a rectangle of backing fabric measuring 16" x 15"

Cut a rectangle of backing fabric measuring 16" x 4 ½"

## Pink/Green Pillow with Border

Cut a square of fabric for the pillow front measuring 13 ½" x 13 ½"

Cut a square of thin batting measuring 15 ½" x 15 ½".

Cut a square of batting measuring 15 ½" x 15 ½" (this fabric is the backing for the pillow front; it will be inside the pillow and will not be visible)

Cut a rectangle measuring 16" x 15"

Cut a rectangle measuring 16" x 4 ½"

Cut 44 squares measuring 2"x 2"

Cut 4 squares measuring 1 ½" x 1 ½"; cut in half diagonally to create 8 triangles. (If you would like to include more colors in these corner sections, cut more squares and throw away leftover triangles)

## Sieglinde's Secret

*For the design on the next page, you will want to appliqué your own special letter in place of my letter K. You can create your own letter in a similar style to mine, add seam allowance, and appliqué as usual. Or, for additional letters, refer to my book Mother Earth's ABC, which offers templates for every letter of the alphabet, both upper case and lower case. For a super-quick way to transfer letters, I have also published Mother Earth's ABC: Phototransfer Pack & CD. Use this to digitally print letters onto fabric sheets. Look at the back of the book for more information on both these products.*

*Note that the girl's face, hair, neck, and hands are embroidered, not appliquéd. So are the bumblebee, the long green stems, many of the smaller green leaves, and some of the flower centers. Look carefully at the photograph to see which pieces are embroidered; you will not need to cut appliqués for these pieces.*

**2** Off-white and teal pillows: On the pillow front fabric, mark a line 1 ¼" inwards from the edge around the entire pillow. The appliqué design will fall inside this border. Proceed to Step 7.

**3** Pink/green pillow: Arrange the color squares into groupings of 10 in a color sequence that pleases you. Sew the blocks together by hand or machine so that you have four long strips made up of 10 blocks each.

**4** Arrange the remaining square and the triangles into sets of three as shown. Sew together along the short edges.

**5** Right sides together and aligning seam allowance, position a unit from the previous step at each corner of the pillow front. With a ¼" seam allowance, sew across the diagonal to attach. Turn under ¼" seam allowance along the short diagonal and appliqué this edge to the pillow front.

**6** Right sides together, pin a border strip to one edge of the pillow, starting at the center and working outwards. Sew in place by hand or machine. In the same way, add the remaining three borders.

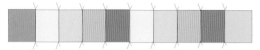

Step 3  Make four

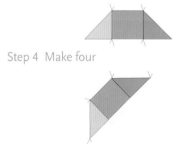

Step 4  Make four

Step 5  Sew at each corner

# Appliqués and Embroidery

**7** Trace and transfer all the motifs and designs from the master template onto the background for the pillow front. Following the directions on pages 12 to 13, trace carefully to make sure you catch every single detail. Continually check against the master template to ensure accuracy.

**8** Adding ⅛" seam allowance, cut appliqués for the girl's dress and the shoes of the girl in pink. Sew the feet in place first, then the dress (see page 13 for help with appliqué).

**9** Complete the layered embroidery of the child's faces, hair, and hands. (For help with layered embroidery, see page 14.) With black thread, carefully add the children's eyes, brows, mouths, and lips, as in the photograph. For the purple girl, add three French knots for buttons (see page 16).

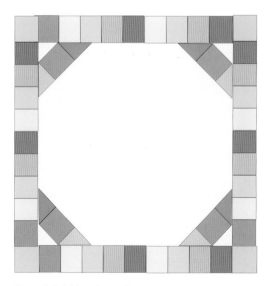

Step 6  Add border strips

*Note that the girl's face, hair, neck, and hand are embroidered, not appliquéd. So are the bumblebee, the butterfly, the long green stems, many of the smaller green leaves, and some of the flower centers. Look carefully at the photograph to see which pieces are embroidered; you will not need to cut appliqués for these pieces.*

**10** Cut appliqués for the flowers. Look carefully at the photographs to see which areas are appliqué and which are embroidered. Most of the flower petals and the larger leaves are appliqué; most of stems, smaller leaves, flower buds and flower centers are embroidered. Refer to the photographs to determine the proper sequence for sewing each appliqué flower piece in place. Complete the appliqué before beginning embroidery.

**11** For the teal pillow, complete the appliqué of the letter, the butterfly, the snail, the ladybug. Complete the appliqué flowers and leaves on top of the letter. For the green/pink pillow, appliqué flowers at each corner, overlapping onto the border.

**12** Check each photograph carefully and also check the master template to make sure you have completed all the appliqué. Sometimes it may be difficult to tell which details are appliqué and which are embroidered; look through the book to find every photograph of your project so that you distinguish appliqué from embroidery.

**13** Complete the embroidered bees and butterflies (see page 14). Use stem stitch and green embroidery thread to complete the blades of grass.

**14** With single-strand black embroidery thread and stem stitch, outline all elements of the design completed so far. Begin by outlining around each child's body, face, hair, and hands. Outline the butterflies and bugs, adding the antennae and wing patterns. Add a line of black stem stitch next to each blade of grass. Study the photograph to see exactly where to outline.

**15** Continually check against the master templates and photographs to ensure accuracy. Lay your tracings over the project and make sure there are no design motifs or details you have missed. Make sure every motif is outlined with black embroidery thread.

## Sieglinde's Secret

*If you were able to look at the back of one of my appliqué projects, you would see that I leave many areas unquilted. Rather than struggle with appliqué seams, I quilt only the open areas of the background, between and around the motifs. Since my projects are often quite small, I work without a hoop or frame, quilting on my lap. Do whatever is comfortable for you!*

# Quilting

**16** Lay out the backing for the pillow front on a table top, and position the batting then the pillow front over it, smoothing each layer out as you go. Pin the layers together, using one pin at least every square inch. Baste the entire piece, holding the layers together, and remove the pins.

**17** Off-white pillow: With yellow embroidery thread, make French knots through all layers, exactly ½" apart (see page 16). I usually judge by eye to avoid marking. Begin at the edge of the appliqué motifs and work outwards to the marked border until all French knots are complete. Do not stitch on top of motifs, just on the open areas of the pillow. Do not stitch within the border you marked in Step 2.

**18** Pink/green pillow: With pink embroidery thread, make simple cross stitches through all layers, exactly ½" apart (see page 17). I usually judge by eye to avoid marking. Begin at the edge of the appliqué motif and work outwards to the marked border until all French knots are complete. Do not stitch on top of motifs, just on the open areas of the pillow. Do not stitch within the border you marked in Step 2.

**19** Teal pillow: The quilting pattern for all the open areas around the appliqués is a ½" square grid, set on point (see diagram opposite). I usually quilt without marking, but if you need to, lightly mark the pattern onto the open areas of the quilt top using a water-soluble marker. Do not quilt over the appliqués or the embroidery.

**20** Using stem stitch and embroidery floss, stitch around the entire pillow front, 1 ½" inwards from the edge (along the border line you marked in Step 2). Stitch through all layers.

# Pillow Back

**21** With the large backing piece from Step 1, fold one edge inwards by ½" then by 1". Press, then sew along both folds. Repeat with the small backing piece from Step 1.

## Sieglinde's Secret

*Because batik fabrics, which I used for the background, the cameos, and the appliqués, are hard to needle, I always use the thinnest batting I can find. My preference is Mountain Mist's 100 percent cotton batting, which needles very easily.*

**22** Right sides and raw edges together, align the small backing piece with the bottom edge of the pillow as shown. Pin then sew along one short side, the long side, and then the other short side. Turn right side out.

**23** Right sides and raw edges together, align the large backing piece with the rest of the pillow. It will overlap the small backing piece by about 1". Pin then sew around all three sides. Turn right side out.

**24** Teal and off-white pillows only: Working from the front and sewing through all layers, use stem stitch and embroidery thread to sew around the entire border marked in Step 2.

**25** Either attach three pieces of Velcro to close the pillow, or make buttonholes and sew on three buttons.

**26** Stuff with a pillow form or soft batting.

Quilting design for the teal pillow

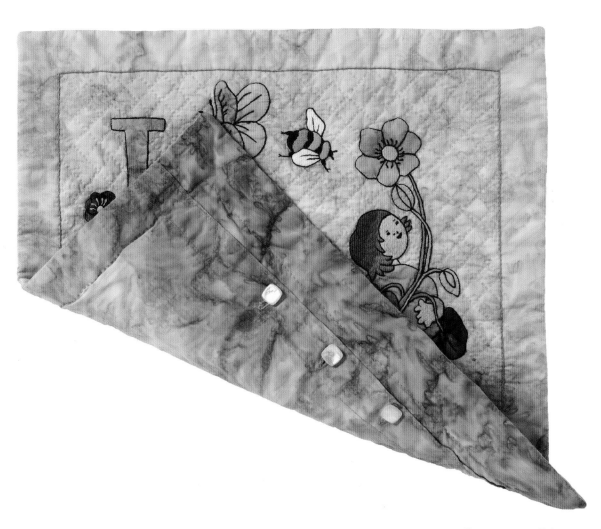

# Summer Bouquet

"They swarm the meadow like little bees,
Dance with dandelions, play among reeds.
Beetles and butterflies delight in the day
If only the Summer would not fade away."

Guess who the little children in the table runner are? My sisters and me! How we loved Summer when we were little. With Oma to watch over us, we would march to the meadows, often taking our handcrafts with us. There I would sit, pretending that God had created everything I could see just for

Finished size: 62" x 16½", including binding

me—the bugs and snails, the frogs and butterflies, and, oh, those glorious flowers! I would crawl on my hands and knees for a closer look, studying just how the petals broke free of the stem, forming their own shapes as they opened up to the sunshine. With my tiny embroidery hoop and a bundle of threads, I would try to recreate the flower exactly as I saw it. Sometimes, I would take my work to Oma. She would look carefully, admiring my new flower and saying it was good but not pretty enough yet. Then she would take out her sharp scissors and carefully cut all my stitches out of the canvas. She would set me to work again, smiling and praising me. At last, she would take a good long look and pronounce my work "pretty." Her lessons have stayed with me throughout my life. Even today, whenever I have completed a task, I look at my projects through Oma's eyes to see if she would decide my work was pretty.

# Materials

All quantities are generous so that you can cut large shapes from a single piece of fabric, wherever possible. You will have plenty of leftover fabric to play with! For the background and appliqués, I use cotton batiks. The slight color variation across the yardage lends a natural feel that is in keeping with the style of the table runner.

Notice that I cut my binding from the same fabric I used for the border, as I wanted it to blend. If you prefer, you can use a contrasting fabric or packages of solid-cover bias binding.

## Background, Border, and Backing

**Background:** 2 yards off-white (you will have leftover fabric)
**Border:** ¾ yard of batik in summer or spring shade
**Backing:** 1 yard. I saved fabric by sewing together two pieces from the same yard. If it is important to you to have no seam, buy two yards of backing fabric.
**Binding:** 5 yards single-fold bias binding or 1" bias strips in border fabric

## Appliqués

**Dresses:** Large scraps of purple, light blue, red, and gold
**Shoes:** Scraps of green or brown
**Flowers and foliage:** Scraps in multiple colors, plus at least four shades of green
**Bugs and butterflies:** Scraps in multiple colors

## Plus

**Embroidery:** Single-ply embroidery thread in cream, beige, tan, light brown, dark brown, black, gold, pink, yellow, green, red, orange, magenta, lilac, and whatever additional colors you please
**Batting:** ¼ yard very thin batting (see *Sieglinde's Secret* on page 35)

If you decide to make table mats to match your table runner, be sure to check the materials list on page 66 to be certain that you have enough fabric. Together, the table runner and table mats make a beautiful gift for a Spring party or bridal shower.

*Note:* See page 11 for help in choosing fabrics.

Summer Bouquet

# Prepare Background

**1** Cut a rectangle of off-white fabric measuring 58 ½" x 20 ½". This includes ¼" seam allowance.

**2** On the back, lightly mark a line across the narrow width of the rectangle, 6 ¾" in from the edge. Repeat at the other end of the fabric.

**3** Fold the fabric in half lengthwise, right side in. On a flat surface, lay a straight-edge ruler diagonally across the fabric from A to B. If necessary, pin the layers together to avoid shifting, then cut through both layers diagonally. Repeat at the other end. Open out.

**4** Fold the fabric in half widthwise. On the back, mark a line across the width of the fabric at the center. Open out. Mark the top center edge of the fabric (point C in the diagram). Measure 4" inwards from the edge and mark at the center line (point D). Measure 4" to the left of point D and mark (point E). With a straight rule and rotary cutter or with sharp scissors, carefully cut from C to E.

**5** Cut away along the horizontal of the fabric, 4" inwards from the edge, all the way to the far left of the fabric at point A.

**6** Repeat Steps 4 and 5, this time on the right side of the center line.

**7** Repeat the previous steps, this time working on the bottom edge of the fabric.

**8** On the right side of the fabric, mark a line ¼" from the edge around all sides. This marks the seam allowance.

Step 2 Mark 6¼" in from edges

Step 3 Fold lengthwise; cut diagonal

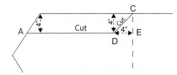

Step 4 Open out; mark left side

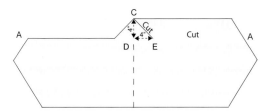

Steps 4 and 5 Cut left side; mark right side

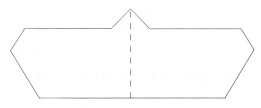

Step 6 Cut right side

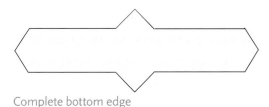

Complete bottom edge

# Transfer Designs

**9** Trace and transfer all the motifs and designs from the master template onto the background. Following the directions on page 12, trace carefully to make sure you catch every single detail. Continually check against the master template to ensure accuracy.

**10** Adding ⅛" seam allowance, cut appliqués for the dresses and shoes of the four girls. Appliqué the shoes in place first, followed by each of the dresses (see page 13 for help with appliqué). Cut appliqués for the large flowers the girls are holding and sew them in place. For the girl in purple, the large purple and white petals are appliquéd, as well as the large green-brown leaf; the rest is embroidery. For the girl in blue, the blue petals and the four green leaves are appliqués. For the girl in red, the red flower piece only is appliquéd. For the girl in gold, the gold flower only is appliqué.

**11** Complete the layered embroidery of the children's faces, hair, necks, and hands (see page 14). With black thread, carefully add the children's eyes, brows, mouths, and lips, as in the photograph. Complete the embroidery of the stems, leaves and flowers. Notice that there are French knots on all four dresses as well as on the blue, red, and gold flowers (see page 16).

**12** Complete the rest of the embroidery, including all the long flower stems, the leaves, and the flower buds and stamens. Use stem stitch with green thread to embroider the blades of grass at the feet of the children (see page 19).

**13** With single-strand black embroidery thread and stem stitch, outline all elements of the design completed so far. Begin by outlining around each child's body, face, hair, and hands. Add a line of black stem stitch next to each blade of grass. Study the photograph to see exactly where to outline.

**14** Move on to another portion of the design. I recommend working on the largest motifs first, such as the large flower clusters. Look carefully at the photographs to determine which portions are appliquéd and which are embroidered. If you have

## Sieglinde's Secret

*I prefer to completely finish tracing and transferring the image to fabric before I begin any sewing. If you are less patient and can't wait to pick up your needle, complete the main figures in the design, such as the children's bodies. Next, choose another distinct area of the design to concentrate on, such as one of the faces or a clump of flowers. Mark your chosen area completely, then start sewing. When you are done, move on to another distinct area of the design.*

not done so already, carefully trace and transfer the designs to the fabric (see page 12). Complete the appliqué first, followed by embroidery, stem stitch embroidery, French knots and other detailing. With single-strand black embroidery thread and stem stitch, outline all elements of the design.

**15** In the same way, complete appliqué, embroidery and outlining for the rest of the design. Continually check against the master template and the photographs to ensure accuracy. Lay your tracings over the table runner and make sure there are no design motifs or details you have missed. Make sure every motif is outlined with black embroidery thread.

## Add Borders

**16** Since sewing on so many appliqués can slightly change the size of the background fabric you are working with, measure your project where the straight horizontal borders will go (measure through the middle of the piece rather than the edge, since the edges tend to stretch). Cut four strips of fabric to match this measurement, plus an extra 4". (This should be about 24", but check to make sure.) The width of each strip will be 2", including seam allowance. Cut four strips measuring 14" x 2" and four strips measuring 8" x 2".

**17** Pin the long borders to the table runner. The borders are slightly longer than needed, to allow for mitering of the border. Pin at the center first, working outwards toward each edge. There should be about 1 ½" or more of border fabric overhanging at each edge. Sew each border strip in place, leaving the overlapping fabric unstitched.

**18** Pin then sew the short 7" strips to the center of the table runner, top and bottom. As before, there will be an extra 1 ½" or more of border fabric at either end. Sew three 45-degree miters to join the borders. (See miter triangle on page 85.)

**19** Pin then sew the 14" x 2" strips to diagonal ends of the table runner. There will be an extra 1 ½" or more of border fabric at either end. Miter the corners to neatly join the border pieces. Turn the table runner over and trim off any excess fabric at the miters.

## Sieglinde's Secret

*Look at the borders as an opportunity to give your table runner its own unique look. When you have finished or almost finished the appliqués and embroidery, take your project to your local quilting or fabric store. Lay it on top of a wide variety of fabrics to see which look you like best. If you wish, choose an altogether different fabric for the binding, rather than matching it to the border.*

**20** Check the size of your table runner again, measuring across the center, horizontally and vertically. Cut a rectangle of backing fabric that matches these measurements, plus an extra inch on all sides. The rectangle will be about 62" x 25", but measure to make sure. (You may need two piece two lengths of fabric together to have the correct 62" width.) Cut a layer of batting with the same measurements. Trim the diagonal corners of both backing and batting to match the corners of the quilt top.

# Quilting

**21** Lay out the backing on a table top, and position the batting then the quilt top over it, smoothing each layer out as you go. Pin the layers together, using one pin at least every square inch. Baste the entire quilt, holding the layers together and remove the pins.

**22** The quilting pattern for all the open areas around the appliqués and is a 1" grid, set on point. I usually quilt without marking, but if you need to, lightly mark the pattern onto the open areas of the quilt top using a water-soluble marker. Do not quilt over the appliqués or the embroidery. The border is not quilted.

**23** Using stem stitch and embroidery floss in gold, pink, green and brown, embroider over the top of the quilting stitches. (These embroidery stitches go through the top layer only, not through the batting or backing.) Embroider rows of gold first, then butt a row of pink next to each one. Do the same with green and brown for opposing diagonal rows.

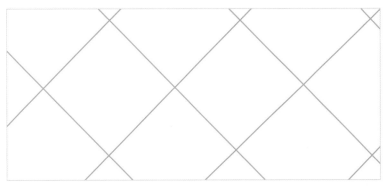

Quilting design

## Sieglinde's Secret

*Because batik fabrics, which I used for the background, the cameos, and the appliqués, are hard to needle, I always use the thinnest batting I can find. My preference is Mountain Mist's 100 percent cotton batting, which needles very easily.*

Summer Bouquet

**24** Using stem stitch and black embroidery floss, stitch on top of the seam between the off-white background and the border.

# Binding

**25** Cut a 1" bias strip of border fabric. Sew bias pieces together to form one long strip, long enough to go all around the outside edge of the table runner. Fold the strip in half lengthwise and press, matching the raw edges exactly. Leave about a 3" to 4" unfolded at one end.

**26** By hand or machine, start to attach the folded end of the strip to the left most tip. Sew around the entire table runner and around each diagonal corner.

**27** Once you get to about 4" to 6" from the end, open the bias strip. Measure how much of the strip is still needed. Trim to the correct length, plus ¼". Turn that ¼" under, fold in half again and fingerpress. Sew the end in place, slightly overlapping the starting point.

**28** Fold the unsewn long edge of the bias toward the back of the table runner and attach with small appliqué stitches.

When you are finished, be sure to add a label to the back of your table runner so that everyone knows that you made it. Either write or embroider your name and the date you completed the project. If you are making a gift of the table runner, you can always add a special message, such as "To my favorite niece in celebration of her wedding." The label will make the gift all the more precious, particularly when it is handed down to the next generation.

## Sieglinde's Secret

*If you were able to look at the back of one of my appliqué projects, you would see that I leave many areas unquilted. Rather than struggle with appliqué seams, I quilt only the open areas of the background, between and around the motifs. Since my projects are often quite small, I work without a hoop or frame, quilting on my lap. Do whatever is comfortable for you!*

I like to imagine that this little table runner is a delightful way to bring the outside indoors. Even on the gloomiest days of Winter, I enjoy brightening my dining table in this way. There is no need to buy flowers for your special luncheon visitors, since they are already here! If your visitors are your children or grandchildren, just set the table runner out on the floor with cushions—and remember to lay places for dolls and other special friends.

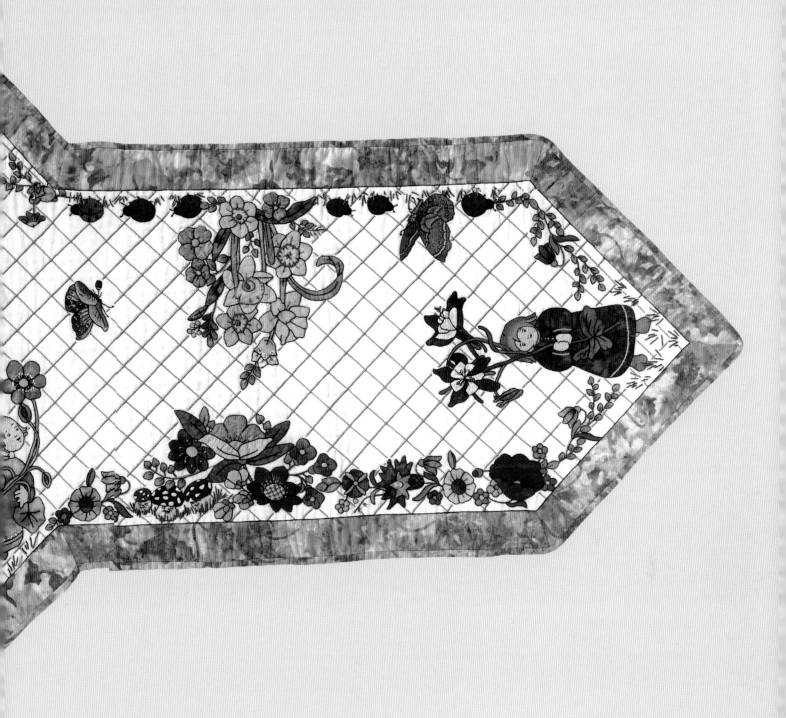

# Table Mats

"Deep in the woods, all cloaked in green,
Flowers blossom. What a wondrous scene!
A violet hides behind a tree,
Scared by a snail, so strange to see."

By the time I was ten years old, the war was over and my hometown in southern Germany became somewhat normal once more. There was much work to be done to restore our little community and find our way in a world that had changed. Everyone, even the children, was called on to help.

Having spent

Finished size: 17" x 12", including binding

many years under my grandmother Oma's tutelage, I now excelled at needlework. My parents were asked if I might join the ladies in church whose task it was to repair the beautiful embroidered robes that our priests wore during mass. My parents were happy to volunteer my help, as it would keep me out of trouble after school. The ladies were all elderly; their fingers were curled and their eyesight was failing. So guess what I got to do? I was allowed to work on the most delicate repairs. Combining the expertise of the older ladies with the agility of my young hands, I learned embroidery stitches I had never seen before. I also learned how to combine colors in beautiful and surprising ways. I was taught by masters of the art and will always be grateful to them.

# Materials

All quantities are generous so that you can cut large shapes from a single piece of fabric, wherever possible. You will have plenty of leftover fabric to play with! For the background and appliqués, I use cotton batiks. The slight color variation across the yardage lends a natural feel that is in keeping with the style of the project.

**Background:** ½ yard or fat quarter of off-white fabric per table mat (you will have leftover fabric)
**Batting:** ¼ yard very thin batting per table mat
**Backing** 2 yards
**Binding:** 2 yards single-fold bias binding or 1" bias strips of backing fabric per table mat

## Appliqués

**Dress:** Large scrap in desired color
**Shoes:** Scraps of green (the feet of the girl in purple are embroidered, not appliquéd)
**Flowers, stems, and leaves:** Scraps in multiple colors, including shades of green
**Butterflies:** Scraps in multiple colors (note that only two of the butterflies are appliqué; the others are embroidered)

## Plus

**Embroidery:** Single-ply embroidery thread in black, gold, pink, yellow, green, red, orange, magenta, lilac, and whatever additional colors you please

*Note:* See page 11 for help in choosing fabrics.

# Prepare Background

**1** Cut a rectangle of off-white fabric measuring 18" x 12 ½". Use a saucer, coffee mug or other round object to mark a gentle curve at each corner. Cut along your marking to round off the corners. Repeat with backing fabric and batting.

**2** On the right side, mark a line ¼" from the edge around all sides. This marks the seam allowance.

# Transfer Designs

**3** Trace and transfer all the motifs and designs from the master template onto the background. Following the directions on page 12, trace carefully to make sure you catch every single detail. Continually check against the master template to ensure accuracy.

# Appliqués and Embroidery

**4**  Adding ⅛" seam allowance, cut appliqués for the dresses and shoes of the girls (note, the feet of the girl in purple are embroidered, not appliqués). Appliqué the shoes in place first, followed by each of the dresses (see page 13 for help with appliqué).

**5**  Complete the layered embroidery of the children's faces, hair, and hands, plus the feet of the girl in purple. (For help with layered embroidery, see page 14.) With black thread, carefully add the children's eyes, brows, mouths, and lips, as in the photograph. Complete the embroidery on the girl's dress (pink girls only).

**6**  Cut appliqués for the large flowers the girl is holding and sew them in place. For the kneeling girl in pink, note that the stems are appliqué and the leaves are embroidered; for the other girl in pink, the large green leaf and the pink and yellow petals are appliqué, but the flower stamens, buds, and stem are embroidered; for the girl in red, the red flower and the green bud

are appliqué; for the girl in purple, the purple petals and the green leaves are appliqué.

**7** If your are making the mat with the pink girl photographed on page 70, cut appliqués for the butterflies (see templates on page 82). All the other butterflies are embroidery only. Sew the appliqués, then complete the embroidery.

**8** With single-strand black embroidery thread and stem stitch, outline all elements of the design completed so far. Begin by outlining around each child's body, face, hair, and hands. Outline the butterflies and add the antennae and wing patterns. Add a line of black stem stitch next to each blade of grass. Study the photograph to see exactly where to outline.

**9** Continually check against the master templates and photographs to ensure accuracy. Lay your tracings over the quilt and make sure there are no design motifs or details you have missed. Make sure every motif is outlined with black embroidery thread.

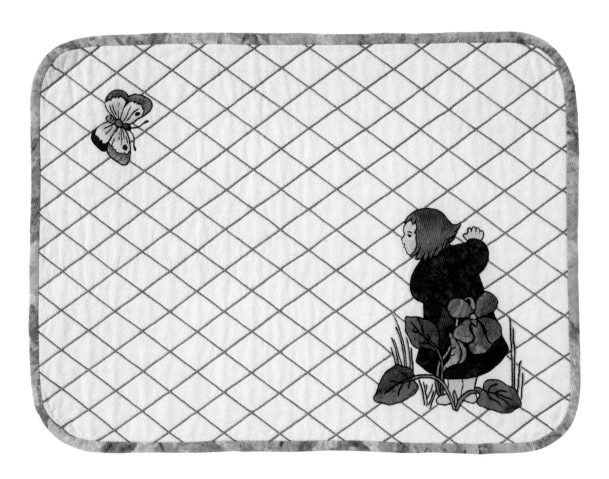

# Quilting

**10** Lay out the backing on a table top, and position the batting then the table mat over it, smoothing each layer out as you go. Pin the layers together, using one pin at least every square inch. Baste the entire quilt, holding the layers together and remove the pins.

**11** The quilting pattern for all the open areas around the appliqués and is a 1" diamond grid. I usually quilt without marking, but if you need to, lightly mark the pattern onto the open areas of the quilt top using a water-soluble marker. Do not quilt over the appliqués or the embroidery.

**12** Using stem stitch and embroidery floss in two complimentary colors, embroider over the top of the quilting stitches. Embroider all rows in your first choice of color, then butt a row of your second color next to each one.

# Binding

**13** Cut a 1" bias strip of border fabric. Sew bias pieces together to form one long strip, long enough to go all around the outside edge of the mat. Fold the strip in half lengthwise and press, matching the raw edges exactly. Leave about a 3" to 4" unfolded at one end.

**14** By hand or machine, start to attach the folded end of the strip to the mat. Sew around the entire mat and around each curved corner.

**15** Once you get to about 4" to 6" from the end, open the bias strip. Measure how much of the strip is still needed. Trim to the correct length, plus ¼". Turn that ¼" under, fold in half again and fingerpress. Sew the end in place, slightly overlapping the starting point.

**16** Fold the unsewn long edge of the bias toward the back of the mat and attach with small appliqué stitches.

Quilting design

# Templates

I left Germany
as a young woman and now
live in the United States.  It would
make me very happy to think that today's
young children might learn some of those old
German techniques from me in this wonderful
country. When I was just four years old, I made
up my mind to move here. You see, a young
soldier saved my life. When I asked my
mother where he had come from, she told
me he was American. I promptly
announced that

Off-White Pillow (see page 42)

Match up the two pieces where they overlap,
tape together, then trace to make your
master template.

I would go to America as soon as I grew up. I have raised my family of four children, five grandchildren, and three great-grandchildren here, and I have never for a moment regretted that decision.

# Pink/Green Pillow with Border (see page 46)

Match up the two pieces where they overlap and tape together. Add a corner piece at each corner. Trace to make your master template.

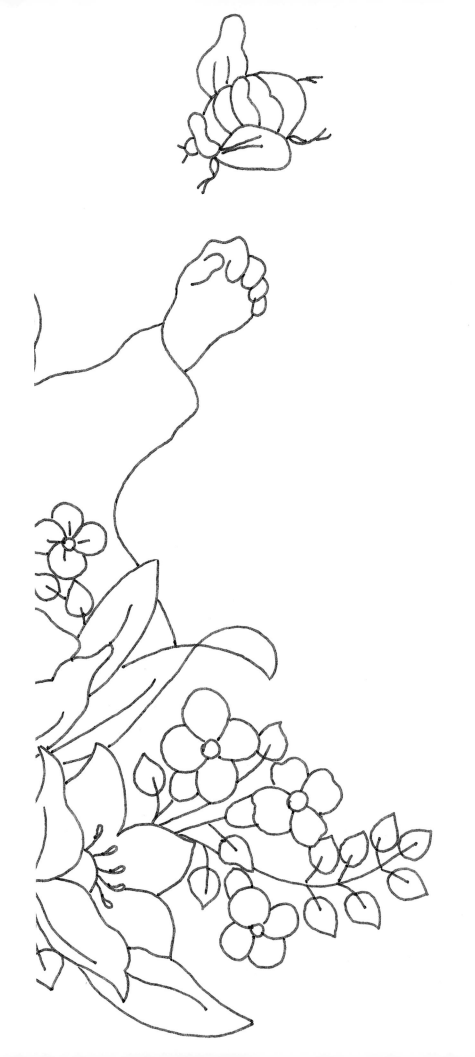

Match up the three pieces where they overlap, tape together,
then trace to make your master template.

## Table Mat (see page 69)

Trace every part of the image to create your master template, positioning the butterfly at top left.

# Table Mat (see page 70)

Trace every part of the image to create your master
template, positioning the butterfly at top left.

## Table Mat (see page 67)

Trace every part of the image to create your master template, positioning the butterfly at top left.

## Table Mat (see page 68)

Trace every part of the image
to create your master template,
positioning the butterfly at top left.

## Miter Triangles

Use the miter triangles to mark diagonal lines for the miters on the borders. Copy or trace onto stiff card and cut out the triangle. Line up the horizontal and vertical edges on the fabric, then lightly mark the diagonal line. Cut along the diagonal.

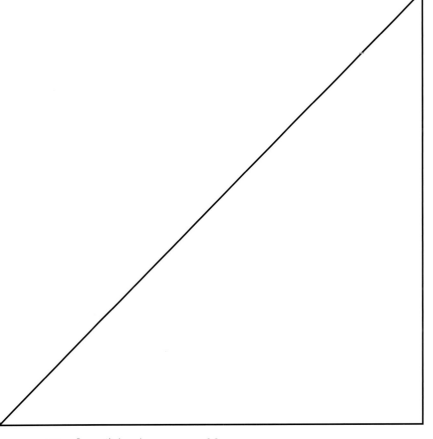

Miter for quilt border, see page 36

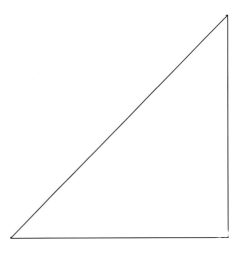

Miter for table runner border, see page 58

*Sieglinde's Secret*

*There are dozens of books available to help you with appliqué, including many by Elly Sienkiewicz. For a basic guide to embroidery, try* Elegant Stitches *by Judith Baker Montano. Jinny Beyer's wonderful book* Quiltmaking by Hand *will help you when it comes to quilting and binding your projects. Another helpful resource is* That Perfect Stitch *by Dierdre McElroy.*

SIBYLLE VON OLFERS

# MOTHER EARTH
## AND HER CHILDREN
### A Quilted Fairy Tale

ILLUSTRATIONS SIEGLINDE SCHOEN SMITH ❦ TRANSLATION JACK ZIPES

MOTHER EARTH'S

ABC

A Quilter's Alphabet

INSPIRED BY *Mother Earth and Her Children*

Sieglinde Schoen Smith

Includes CD plus 5 Quality Fabric sheets

Photo Transfer Pack & CD

MOTHER EARTH'S

ABC

Sieglinde Schoen Smith

### An Appliqué Alphabet As Easy As ABC

- CD with hi-res .tif and .gif image files
- Letters A to Z in upper case and lower case
- Five background images
- 5 top-quality fabric sheets (200 thread count)
- Washable and colorfast
- Easy to sew or fuse

# MOTHER EARTH AND HER CHILDREN
by Sieglinde Schoen Smith

Puzzle size: 27" x 16.5" (68.5 cm x 42 cm)
Poster size: 27" x 16.5" (68.5 cm x 42 cm)

## 750 Piece Jigsaw Puzzle and Poster

MOTHER EARTH'S
QUILT SAMPLER

Appliqué Patterns Inspired by *Mother Earth and Her Children*

Sieglinde Schoen Smith

# Also by Sieglinde Schoen Smith

*Mother Earth and Her Children: A Quilted Fairy Tale*

A charming picture book for young children, celebrating the miracles of nature in the changing seasons. Winner of the American Horticultural Society's Growing Good Kids Book Award.
ISBN: 978-1933308-18-0, 32 pages, hardcover with jacket

*Mother Earth's Quilt Sampler: Appliqué Patterns Inspired by Mother Earth and Her Children*

Four small wall hangings each portraying a different season of the year. Complete, full-size templates included.
ISBN: 978-1933308-22-7, 60 pages, plus shrink-wrapped template pack

*Mother Earth's ABC: A Quilter's Alphabet and Storybook*

A delightful romp from A to Z telling the story of a seed's miraculous Spring awakening. Beautiful appliqué letters are ready to trace and sew into quilting projects.
ISBN: 978-1933308-20-3, 40 pages, hardcover with jacket

*Mother Earth's ABC: Phototransfer Pack and CD*

An easy way to reproduce Sieglinde's illustrated alphabet: ready to resize, arrange, and print onto fabric sheets. Requires basic design or picture editing program (pre-installed on most newer computers).
UPC: 8-82383-00029-3, CD plus 5 fabric sheets

*Mother Earth's Jigsaw Puzzle and Poster*

Recreate the images in Sieglinde's award-winning quilt, one puzzle piece at a time. Includes a folded poster of Mother Earth and Her Children.
ISBN: 978-1933308-24-1, 750 piece jigsaw puzzle plus poster (27" x 16½")

For more information contact Breckling Press
at 630 941 0949 (800-951-7836) or visit www.brecklingpress.com

## About the Author

Sieglinde Schoen Smith dazzled the quilt world when her hand-made, hand-embroidered quilt, Mother Earth and Her Children, won America's top prize at International Quilt Festival. This masterful work captured the hearts of quilters and inspired Sieglinde to write a children's picture book, also titled *Mother Earth and Her Children*. The book was awarded the American Horticultural Society's Growing Good Kids Book Award. Sieglinde is a master quilter, an expert embroider, and a gifted artist. She has taught her unique sewing techniques at national and regional quilt festivals as well as at numerous quilt shops in her home state and across the country. Sieglinde lives in Carlisle, Pennsylvania.